Schooner Press

Cloud Computing 101
By James D. Michelson

THIS EDITION IS AVAILABLE FOR BULK SALES. PLEASE CONTACT SCHOONER PRESS IN THE UNITED STATES AT:

sales@schoonerpress.com • www.schoonerpress.com

Submissions for Publication

Schooner Press accepts unsolicited submissions from authors without Representation. Submit cover letter, synopsis, and entire text to editor@schoonerpress.com. Simultaneous submissions are not accepted. Submitted materials will not be returned.

Library of Congress Cataloging-in-Publication Data

Michelson, James D

Cross Media Marketing 101 / James D. Michelson

ISBN-13: 978-0-9890261-5-4

Cloud Computing 101

An essential technical tool for small and medium enterprises

By James D. Michelson

Contents

Forward

The goal of this work is simple – to understand the modern way to use those glowing boxes that clutter desks, fill briefcases and stuff pockets. The content is based on decades of global sales calls, information technology projects and proposals for both public and private sector clients. These efforts have laid bare the substantial gaps in the information technology knowledge base of many decision makers in virtually every vertical. This book will help fill those gaps.

The first belief that most executives have and that must be immediately dispelled is that the situation of their firm or their position is unique. It's not. Just accept that fact and let's move on. In any industry from for profits to quasi-governmental agencies the organization needs to generate revenue, provide goods or services and maintain clients or constituents while satisfying stakeholders. There are no exceptions. Every enterprise has the exact same challenges to overcome and they are universal.

There are no hidden agendas in the content of this work and the conclusions are based on lessons learned from Fortune 5000, critical infrastructure facilities, sport authorities, sovereign states and the worlds' 1% from their mega yachts to their personal residences. The industry has reached the inescapable conclusion that with very few exceptions computing power will return to its roots and be executed at centralized locations. This change is already well underway and may be over before many users realize the consequences and opportunity costs. The cloud that your data accesses may be sending proprietary information globally, but that device in your hand and on your desk will not, and should not, be doing the heavily lifting.

There are no exists from this aircraft. So please sit back, put your tray tables into the upright and locked opposition and enjoy the flight. "You don't have to like it, but you can't ignore it."[1]

---

[1] The two Swedes. From ShowTime's unfortunately short-lived *Happyish* sitcom that nails the business world perfectly.

Introduction

In one day in 2015 three separate computer security incidents occurred simultaneously at the New York Stock Exchange, United Airlines and the Wall Street Journal. It turned out that the immediate speculation of a coordinated cyberattack from a foreign government agency or nefarious activity by anti-globalization fanatics was unfounded. The mere possibility of a coordinated effort brought major concerns to light. First, it demonstrated the massive amount of disruption that organizations can suffer in the event of computer glitches. Second, even large firms with vast information technology resources can be hobbled by the failure to maintain and upgrade basic equipment. The United failure is of particular interest to small and medium enterprises.

United's passengers suffered from canceled flights and missing luggage while the airline lost revenue and was forced to provide substantial payouts to stranded passengers. All of this chaos was caused by a few outdated routers that were expensive to replace and time consuming to upgrade. The nation's second largest carrier was grounded globally, stranding thousands of passengers, all because of a budget decision to defer maintenance. International bad press and the loss of passenger good will, always in short supply for airlines, hurt short term stock performance. There are three key lessons for business leaders in this example.

- Maintaining proprietary equipment is expensive and difficult. Even routine failures can prove to be catastrophic to the enterprise and its operations. It is not only behemoths that face the deferred maintenance and upgrade dilemma. Windows Server 2003 is still the current backbone of many installed computer systems for public and private organizations of all sizes. Microsoft ended support for Windows Server 2003 in July of 2015 which makes these computers particularly vulnerable. The multitude of organizations that have this hardware are unlikely to have inhouse information technology support or the capital budget to replace these legacy systems.

- Expansion, mergers, acquisitions (such as United's merger with Continental in 2014) and a decade's worth of obsolete gear often force technicians to cobble together very disparate systems, data and equipment. This is also a struggle for small and medium sized businesses as the software platform they built their processes on is either no longer in production or have migrated to the cloud.
- United was forced to cancel flights and interrupt their business operations (and that of their passengers and vendors) because there was no back up plan in place for the loss of the computer systems in question. Imagine the chaos that would have ensued if the problem took weeks instead of hours to resolve?

Every size enterprise needs to have backups and a disaster recovery plan for their critical business systems that can be executed in a time frame that allows for acceptable levels of disruption to operations and damage to customer service and satisfaction. While some organizations can adequately support client needs with hours, days or weeks of downtime customer expectations are constantly increasing. Others, such as health care providers, airlines, banks and both web and brick and mortar retailers can never afford to be off line.

A brief history of the universe (of computing)

Unfortunately, I am just old enough to remember the first desktop computer lab installed in my college dormitory at The George Washington University. It consisted of four very snazzy standalone 8086 chip personal computers with a green CRT monitor the size of a 1957 Buick. There was no hard drive but you could load programs. I mainly used WordPerfect off a 5 ¼ inch floppy drive and it took years to make the hand built spellchecker reliable. This was a sweet deal because I didn't have to get dressed and hike across campus to a dumb terminal in the library of the science building to access a mainframe just to write a paper. As my editors will confirm, a typewriter is certainly not an acceptable tool for this author to use. Notes for term papers and thesis were still done the old fashioned way, handwritten on 3 x 5 index cards. The world seems to have come full circle. From mainframe computers with dumb terminals back to devices that access computing power remotely. What happened?

In the beginning…

The history of business computing can be logically divided into eras not by the various technologies and applications available, but rather by the most expensive part of the information technology process. When processing power was the most expensive element it made sense that access to data and chips be remote. When processing power required dedicated rooms and was driven by vacuum tubes it was the most expensive part of the equation to build and operate.

When processing power dropped in cost with the wide availability of the microchip the most expensive input quickly became bandwidth. The amount of data businesses were starting to process required speed and low cost and neither of these were available via the phone lines. Businesses moved wholesale into local devices and Bill Gates and Michael Dell got rich.

The 4 Stages of Computing

Era	Principle Technology	Expense Point
Prior to 1988	Main frame computers with dummy terminals	Processing power
1988 to 2010	Desktop computing	Connectivity
2010 to present	Cloud computing	Local devices
Future	Algorithms & Display	Intellectual property

When the burden of processing and software ownership became the most expensive piece of the tech puzzle the market naturally shifted back to computing where applications are remotely accessed by users. Hardware, software, updates, upgrades, virus and spam protection, regulatory compliance and other issues quickly add up to significant expenses that can be readily shared among users in a cloud environment. It's all just a little bit of history repeating.

It makes sense, all other things being equal, to get the most effective user experience in the cheapest way possible. Anyone who used an early version of Windows may debate the quality of the user experience on that era of PC, but let's accept in principle that it worked out that way.

Future of IT

The next silicon valley billionaire will be the guy who develops a truly user friendly input / output device that doesn't rely on small fixed screens requiring swipes and touches. The basis of this technology is likely to be algorithmic. The vast of amount personally identifiable data that is being collected about users will be grouped together into highly targeted personas and then relevant information, content, products and services can be recommended or automatically engaged by the ghost in the machine.

The logic behind this prediction is that the single most onerous part of smartphone technology are little all these helpful little apps that do one little thing. Fitness information is in one place, restaurant reviews are in another, the bus schedule is in yet another and the weather is someplace else and never where we need them at the right time. Predictive algorithms will figure out what we are likely to need at the moment and then offer suggestions. The Fitbit on my wrist could easily cue up that I have burned 1700 calories and determine a statistically derived suggestion that it is time for lunch.

The algorithm would then note that there is a Whole Foods 365.45 yards away with a lunch special that matches my known preferences for $5.99. The individual inputs are already there and only require better logic and new interface.

Security concerns

By the end of the decade virtually every organization will have shifted their business model from maintaining on site processing power and software. It will have transferred from local operation of servers and software to some version of cloud computing. As these services have become standard operating procedure cloud computing security has become a critical issue for both the private and public sectors. Businesses, consumers and government organizations at all levels must take adequate steps to assure the privacy and security of the data that is transmitted from users to the cloud and back. This topic will covered in great detail.

Challenge assumptions early and often

Be sure that the assumptions the organization is operating under for information technology are true. Too many times I have heard the phrase "you know your business better than I do" when in fact the leaders being addressed know parts of the business very well and others not at all. By the time managers discover that the assumptions of the organization are flawed, or that the market has shifted since the last review, it is often too difficult to recover.

There are still extensive gaps that can be exploited by hackers and criminals as will be explored herein. While not all security threats to data can be eliminated there are steps that can be taken to reduce the likelihood of and mitigate the impact of security breaches. As cloud computing and storage become mainstream users can take proactive steps to protect proprietary or personal information from theft, loss or misuse. Data breaches caused by vulnerabilities in software and systems are not a thing of the past. In 2017 the Cloudfare Security breach exposed data from thousands of websites including many with household names. A bug in the code of the Cloudfare content delivery network allowed cached memory leaks to be indexed and stored by search engines. This vulnerability may have opened usernames and passwords to exploitation. According to analyst Ben Lovejoy:

"This incident underlines the vulnerability of even the most secure services to weaknesses in third-party code. Just yesterday, it was revealed that Apple has cut ties with one of its server suppliers after potential security issues were found in firmware updates. Apple is reportedly working on building its own cloud infrastructure – including servers – to avoid the risk of hardware being compromised either accidentally or deliberately."

The implications of the severity of this and other recent security breaches are significant for all organizations and individuals concerned with cloud computing security.

Take away

Technology is the backbone of every business process in every organization, even those with just a few employees. It is essential for the leadership team to understand just how long mission critical services can be offline and to provide adequate plans for disaster recovery.

The modern hierarchy of needs

Rather than a pyramid, Maslow's Hierarchy of Needs can be considered a temple worshiping the necessities of modern life.

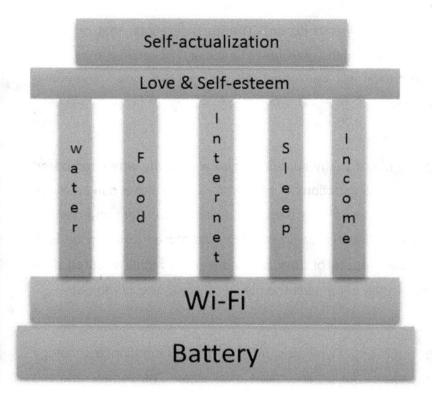

The move to the cloud

Local computing

The move to the cloud is being driven by a number of economic factors that will also have a major effect on security issues. Organizations could decide to maintain a private on-premises system that matched the functionality of cloud computing, but why would a firm desire to do so? The considerations that drive the answer range from the physical to financial. The relative importance of each factor will be measured against the cloud computing environment.

Physical security

The cloud offers vastly superior physical security when compared to local computing options. A server stored in a closet can easily be removed by thieves or a disgruntled employee. Personal devices that have confidential or proprietary data stored on them be lost. The remote storage of data and systems in highly secured data centers virtually eliminates the risk of physical security threats.

Capital expense

Cloud computing eliminates most of the information technology capital expense for organizations of all sizes. The vendor selected provides the physical infrastructure and software licenses required to operate the computing environment. This arrangement allows for the initial launch of the computing system and even subsequent increases in capacity to turn from capital to operating expense. Most businesses and organizations not running on a grant cycle will benefit greatly.

Maintenance and repair

The operational costs of maintaining and repairing infrastructure becomes fixed for organizations utilizing cloud computing. The risks associated with hardware failure, system upgrades, loss of power, data corruption, software updates, security patches and other variables are absorbed by the vendor. The end result is that potential capital expenses from unforeseen needs become a predictable operating expense. The risk is spread by the vendor across multiple clients.

Vendor management

Regardless of the type of cloud computing solution selected the number of vendors that administrators and executives need to manage decreases commensurate with the outsourcing. It is easier to deal with the cloud vendor as a single point of contact rather than multiple vendors for hardware, software, licensing, power, networking and access.

Labor competition and cost

Database administrators, network engineers, software engineers and security specialists become the responsibility of the vendor. These technical employees are in high demand and that demand results in significant compensation. By utilizing these expensive and specially trained personnel across multiple clients the net cost to the organization is less than if they had to employ each. The risk of a disgruntled employee being able to execute a significant theft of data or causing a breach or other loss from internal efforts or by installing malware is also greatly reduced.

Leadership team distraction

The fewer distractions that senior management has in the budgeting, managing and operating of computing systems the more time that can be spent on core business competencies. Oversight that would otherwise be spent on the myriad of information technology systems management tasks can be turned toward practical security matters such as training and audits.

Disaster recovery

The chances of catastrophic failure in a local system are much higher than that of a cloud system. The level of expertise and resources that a dedicated computer services firm will be able to bring to bear in the event of an emergency are likely to be larger and more quickly deployed than by an individual enterprise. The assets available to cloud service providers both in terms of internal capability and access to external resources from equipment and software manufacturers is going to be far greater than for all but a handful of very large, very sophisticated organizations.

Advantages of Cloud Computing over Local Computing

The advantages of cloud computing over inhouse systems are generally accepted to include cost, security, scalability and global access. While cloud computing has many of the same vulnerabilities as local options, they are in many ways easier to control. The advantages and the potential security implications of each follow.

Universal access

Although Virtual Private Networks (VPNs) that allowed remote access to an organization's computing infrastructure have been available for decades they were traditionally slow and inconvenient. Cloud based software runs at speeds comparable to, and oftentimes faster than, those which are locally installed. The computing power of the server is generally far greater than that of the local device and the user device only needs to act as a monitor. The bandwidth to the access device only has to transfer display information so even complex systems can run remotely. The inherent characteristics of cloud computing, including the location of data storage and the physical security of that storage, make cloud systems more secure overall because there is no need for local code or data storage.

Device and operating system agnostic

One of the major advantages of cloud computing is that virtually any program can be run on any operating system that supports web access. This means that an organization's employees can use resources from any device on any screen size ranging from a small smartphone to tablet to laptop computer and be provided with an identical user experience. Because the need to maintain multiple versions of software for various operating systems on multiple platforms can be eliminated by cloud computing, the risk of system vulnerabilities is dramatically decreased.

Data centers

The remote location of a firm's computing power and data storage have several distinct advantages over locally installed systems. First, it is much less likely that a storm hardened data center with multiple redundancies in power, internet access, hardware and personnel will catastrophically fail.

Tier Data Center Levels

Tier 1 – Small Business	99.7% availability 28.8 hours annual downtime Single path of power & cooling No redundant components Lowest cost
Tier 2 – Medium Business	99.75% availability 22 hours annual downtime Single path of power & cooling Some redundancy Lower cost
Tier 3 – Large Business	99.98% availability 1.6 hours annual downtime Multiple paths of power & cooling Fault Tolerant (N+1) Absorb 72 hour power outage
Tier 4 – Enterprise	99.995% availability 0.4 hours annual downtime 2 sources of power & cooling Fault Tolerant (2N+1) Absorb 96 hour power outage

Second, data centers are located in discreet, highly secured facilities that use complex access procedures and feature nifty physical security tricks like trap doors. There are four types of data centers known as tiers that have increasing levels of reliability and calculated uptime. Cost increases with redundancy and the amount of expected downtime.

Physical security

Perhaps the single largest advantage to security made possible by cloud computing is the decrease in physical risk. Lost laptops, smartphones, zip drives and other data storage devices can be easily hacked even by the inexperienced using a variety of commercially available tools.

In a cloud computing environment proprietary data and systems are remotely located and the physical loss of the device is virtually immaterial to security. Data centers layer security protocols into four levels. There are perimeter, facility, computer room and cabinet controls. Perimeter security features physical obstacles such as fences and discreet locations combined with electronic security measures such as alarms and cameras. Facility controls include indoor surveillance for identification and monitoring and multiple identification verification processes. Computer room controls include limiting access to designated individuals, possession of the correct keys or tokens for access, passwords and pins and biometric security such as finger prints and vascular (eye) pattern recognition. Cabinet controls included access restrictions, cabinet locks, surveillance, video monitoring and audit trails.

Data Center security summary

Perimeter	Discreet locations
	Fencing & gates
	Cameras
	Alarms
Facility	Trap door access
	Surveillance
	Multiple identification process
Computer Room	Limited access
	Key and token required
	Password and Pins
	Biometric scanning
Cabinet	Limited access
	Cabinet locks
	Surveillance
	Audits

Redundancy

Redundancy refers to more than the multiple systems such as power and internet connectivity available in a datacenter environment. For a data center, redundancy is defined in terms of the number of redundant systems available for each part of the system. N+1 means there is one redundant system and N+2 means there are two redundant components for each on completely separate feeds for the highest level of availability.

Redundancy is also the security of being able to have duplicates of critical systems always available. This can occur not only in the same data center but also in another. In the event of a major casualty such as data corruption or malware attack a redundant system becomes a practical security option.

Backup

There are two aspects to backup in addition to those discussed in redundancy. First, the use of cloud computing and the vast power and storage of data centers makes copying data for use in the event of a ransomware attack or other security breach more practical and less expensive. Second, the same computing and storage power of multiple data centers makes it less likely that such a backup will fail and that backups will actually be available for use when the time comes.

Rollover

If an organization cannot afford to have mission critical resources offline than a sample backup may be insufficient to serve as a remedy in case of a failure. Rollover allows for a duplicate system to take over operations in a very short time frame in the event the primary system fails. Although this is possible in a local computing environment it is much more expensive and impractical for most organizations to execute. The technical expertise and operation skill to create such a backup system locally is highly specialized and beyond the ability of most information technology departments.

Expertise

There are only so many competent technology experts available. The likelihood is that a dedicated cloud services provider will have the budget and work environment most appealing to professionals in the field. Additionally, because data centers tend to be large and profitable customers for software and hardware manufacturers, these facilities are likely to have the best access to technical support.

Security updates

By having software and data stored in the cloud and managed by others, leadership teams can rely on their third party vendors not only to be more aware of changes but also to process software and hardware updates in a more timely fashion than their inhouse counterparts. The organization's tech team will have security updates for hardware and software as one of many tasks while a datacenter will have this a core competency and a crucial part of not only their business model but contractual obligations. These advantages can be accessed in a variety of possible combinations.

Take Away

The capabilities of modern remote computing services make local installation of hardware and software obsolete and increase the risk of security and downtime.

Cloud Computing

One of the first challenges for organizational leaders to overcome is terminology. Depending on the vendor, their point of view of the world is based on whatever it is they happen to be peddling. Words will have different definitions and get muddled up in marketing speak. There seems to be no end in sight.

One eternally confusing buzz word is solutions. "Complete cloud solutions" means nothing to anyone about anything. Is the provider really talking about handling everything from power generation, bandwidth, hardware, software, maintenance, help desk, wireless connectivity and everything else required to run a modern information technology process? Unless the organization in question is deploying strategic nuclear weapons or something of equal gravity, I seriously doubt it.

To clear things up, almost all providers in information technology fall into one of the following broad categories. The main differentiators are the amount of equipment and licenses the end user owns and the amount of time spent by the enterprise self-managing the various parts of the system. The needs of the organization and the level of risk that the leadership team is comfortable balanced against cost will determine which solution best fits their needs.

It is important for leaders on the senior team to understand that cloud computing is not synonymous with software. In order to accurately assess the cloud computing world it is important to understand the three types of services available and the four ways in which those cloud services can be provided.

Three types of cloud computing systems

Public

Public cloud computing has been common in the United States among consumers for years. Some of the most popular Web 1.0 services such as America Online Line and Excite Mail were early public clouds. In simplest terms, a public cloud uses one database where users are able to access their information from a single source using a username and password. All information is stored together. Public clouds gained acceptance with businesses when software as a service customer relationship management and payroll services caught on and users started storing business data in remote servers owned by third parties.

Private

Private clouds are accessed by only one user group but there are several different definitions of private clouds floating in the marketplace. In some cases, a private cloud may actually share a server that is partitioned off via software to isolate one set of data from another. In another case the servers could share the same rack and infrastructure in a leased data center. In a third case, the servers that power the cloud can be completely physically isolated from all other users in independent racks with proprietary wiring. The difference lies in the level of isolation (security) the firm requires. The more secure the system, the more expense is incurred.

Community Cloud

A community cloud is essentially a private cloud that is accessed by multiple users with a common tie. The arrangement allows for the security and scalability of a private cloud with the flexibility and most of the cost savings of a public cloud. One of the best ways for this type of solution to work is through an umbrella membership organization such as an association, chamber of commerce or even something as small as a sports league. Two example use cases for a community cloud follow.

- Professional Groups: Many professional practices are micro-businesses that have one to ten computer users. Accountants, lawyers, independent insurance agents, financial & estate planners, real estate brokers, massage therapists and personal trainers may all have access to highly confidential personally identifiable health and financial information about their clients. Minimizing the risk of that information getting into nefarious hands is not only a moral and professional obligation but also a very serious legal one. The Health Insurance Portability and Accountability Act (HIPAA), the Data Protection Act and other state and federal legislation make it imperative to have an adequately secure information technology environment regardless of the firm's size. Sole proprietors working directly for clients or other contract vendors may need the ability to provide proof that their access to data meets client expectations. A single lawyer working on a trademark or patent case for reasonably expect to be held to the same data security standards as the largest law practices.

- Not for Profits & Education: Multi-jurisdictional operations, global access to fundraising and other complex data concerns affect not for profits and educational institutions of all sizes. Academic institutions are unique creatures with dozens of budget centers which often have conflicting priorities. That being said, most students require a common set of tools to be successful and a community cloud can provide access to a comprehensive suite of applications for the entire institution or they can be created by school or department.

Any organization can add cloud computing as a member benefit. This can be included as part of the dues or as an additional revenue stream. The smaller the average size member of the organization is the more appealing it will be to the membership.

Type	Equipment Ownership	Management Effort	Difficulty	Cost
Public	No	Low	Low	Low
Private	No	Low	Medium	Medium
Hybrid	Yes	High	High	High

Hybrid

Hybrid clouds use a combination of local and remote computing power. Organizations may choose to maintain highly sensitive or mission critical databases locally while other functions can operate in the cloud. A defense contractor may keep Top Secret design materials in a secure local facility with no connection to the internet while still using commercially available customer relationship management or other productivity applications. The main security concern is that there is no bleed over from the secure to cloud data. This could easily happen as an email attachment.

Cloud Computing Systems Comparisons

Type	Description Infrastructure	Considerations
Public	Available to multiple organizations Offsite location Owned by vendor Highest risk profile Least expensive option	1. How secure is the vendor? 2. How financially stable is the vendor? 3. What other types of organizations use the software? 4. What is the opportunity cost of switching vendors? 5. How easy is data to access and backup? 6. What is the TOS for downtime?
Private	Proprietary to one entity On or offsite location Best risk profile Owned by organization	1. May be difficult to scale 2. Most expensive option 3. If offsite, is hardware physically separated or divided using software?
Hybrid	Mix of multiple cloud system types Allows for both private and public cloud capabilities	1. Merging disparate systems increases complexity 2. Increased need to transfer and normalize data

Four types of cloud computing services

In order of complexity there are three main levels of cloud computing services available. Software as a Service is a single internet application that uses a public cloud setup for multiple users. The service offered can as simple as Gmail or as complex as a full customer relationship management and marketing automation platform like Salesforce. Platform as a Service is a product that provides the infrastructure for cloud computing but leaves the operation and management of the software system to the client while the vendor maintains the hardware and licensing infrastructure. Infrastructure as a Service can form the basis for hybrid or private clouds and IT as a Service outsources an organization's entire information technology function.

Software as a Service (SaaS)

Software as a Service providers offer web accessed applications where data storage is in a public cloud. Instead of having a local device power the code of an application and store the data locally all of the computing power and storage occur on the web. Web mail and message boards were the first generally accepted SaaS applications and they go as far back as AOL. In the last several years virtually every major legacy software provider including Apple, Microsoft, Adobe and others has shifted away from installed applications in favor of the recurring revenue of the cloud model.

Most people in the general public are familiar with Software as a Service even if they do not realize it. In proprietary research conducted by the author, 30% of small and medium enterprises leaders reported not being in the cloud while 98% of the same leaders reported using cloud applications when asked specifically by product name. Gmail, Facebook, LinkedIn and Microsoft Office365 are commonly used SaaS products. Most organizations also utilize industry specific web based software to handle document generation, case management, time and billing, scheduling, shipments, data backup another critical business processes.

In a total SaaS environment (which is generally only used by smaller enterprises) the organization is ultimately responsible for the management of the local information technology setup including end user devices and the local network. The firm also maintains local hardware and operating systems on individual laptops, desktops and mobile devices. This maintenance includes the necessary updates to operating systems, spam filters, antivirus software and other commonly encountered information technology issues. Software as a service applications have a few obvious advantages over locally installed server versions. There are also several key considerations to mind to when selecting if a particular SaaS product or even entire software as a service infrastructure is the best choice for the organization.

Advantages of Software as a Service

The main advantage to Software as a Service is that web applications can usually be used on any supported device that has access to an internet connection. Some devices may require an App to be installed for mobile access on a smartphone or tablet, but many programs can use the web browser as the delivery mechanism. The principle advantages lie in productivity and mobility. The user experience follows from device to device and is essentially the same on a tablet in a coffee shop as it is on a desktop in the office.

Software as a Service products run off the provider's infrastructure remotely. The need to download and install functionality and routine security updates on individual machines is therefore eliminated and this can dramatically reduce the overhead of using any particular application. Automatic, forced and non-optional upgrades are also part of the SaaS model. Providers are only going to have one version of their software running and this can be a blessing or a curse depending on the individual user's point of view. On the one hand, security patches, new functionality and other changes automatically upload but many users prefer things just the way they have always been and loathe change. The author has personally experienced adamant user backlash from seemingly minor changes such as altering the style of a button or modernizing the header fonts on a Software as a Service product.

Web applications that rely on the internet to transfer data rather than the computer's local hard drive to run programs may actually operate faster than the same application installed locally. Since processing power at the server is certain to be vastly better than that available on the local device, performance will often improve regardless of the speed of the web connection. The local device actually becomes an input-output terminal so a cheap tablet can be as fast at running complex business applications as the best power desktop configuration. Complex graphic interfaces such as design software and three dimensional rendering are noted exceptions and there is, at present, still the need for locally installed software to make the SaaS system work.

A common objection to SaaS applications which is completely and wholly inaccurate, despite conventional wisdom, is that the security risk of running an application on the internet is more significant than when running the same application on a standalone computer. While a web application running on a private cloud is inherently more secure than programs running on a public cloud with a shared user database, the chances of hacking or theft are actually far less than if the application is running on a local device. A detailed cloud computing security review will be covered in detail in a later section of this book.

Virtually all software publishers have finally figured out the value of the recurring revenue business model. If the organizations current software is not a SaaS with recurring monthly billing yet, just wait a year. In most cases web applications are significantly more expensive than the installed counterpart over the life of the hardware used. Application licenses were traditionally a onetime purchase bought bundled with the hardware or separately as an aftermarket edition. The application code was downloaded to the device's hard drive and was owned by the purchaser.

Some installed applications have long used a hybrid model where users are charged a monthly fee to operate the installed software that requires access to a remote database to function. This is common a common setup in corporate applications such as finance that remotely access proprietary intellectual property which the publisher updates frequently.

Challenges to Software as a Service

Data ownership

In a SaaS environment, it is critical to read the terms and conditions of the provider. Can your proprietary CRM data be aggregated and sold to third parties? Do you own the right to content once it is uploaded to the provider's servers? As the price of the software application being used approaches zero you can be assured that the level of privacy that can be reasonably expected also approaches zero.

There is no free lunch…

All web applications require an internet connection. If there is not a reliable internet connection available at your location or if the host loses internet connectivity for some reason the application and the information stored in the shared database cannot be accessed. Critical applications or businesses that are time sensitive may be at greater risk. Denial of service attacks targeted at other users or power outages can interrupt operations and prevent access to data.

Regardless of the application being used, organizations need to be certain that the provider has the infrastructure in place to conduct appropriate backups. Confirm that the backup schedule meets the business requirements of the organization. Does the vendor backup user data in real time, hourly, daily, weekly, monthly or ever? In the event of a disaster from mechanical, natural or terrorist activity how long will it take for the provider to bring the backup online? Some

SaaS applications feature instant rollover to an unaffected data center while for others it may take hours, days or weeks.

Google Docs and Microsoft Office365 probably have this covered within reasonable limits but there are thousands of small shops which may struggle with the cost of disaster recovery planning, implementation and testing. Some may never have actually tried executing whatever disaster recovery measures are intended to be used. Be sure to ask for proof before committing to a business application that can cause the enterprise significant harm if the application is not available.

Cloud Computing Services Comparison

Type	Server Ownership	Server Effort	Difficulty	Cost
Traditional	Yes	High	High	High
SaaS	No	None	Low	Low
PaaS	No	High	High	High
IaaS	No	High	High	High
ITaaS	No	None	Low	Medium

Platform as a Service (PaaS)

Platform as a Service can is the infrastructure that allows organizations to create and deploy web applications without the expense of buying and maintaining the software and infrastructure that allows it to run. Most Platform as a Service providers offer scalable access to tools that allow software teams to develop, deploy, load balance, and manage billing and subscriptions for their products or internal proprietary applications. These vendors essentially handle the hardware and load balancing portion of the business.

Infrastructure as a Service (IaaS)

Infrastructure as a Service firms provide data center functionality that is maintained by the leasing business. These can take the form of either hybrid or private clouds. Amazon Web Services is a good example of an Infrastructure as a Service. Amazon provides hardware and technicians in one of their vast data centers and the organization contracting for the platform maintains the software and configuration of their system.

Responsibility comparison

Traditional	IaaS	PaaS	SaaS	ITaaS
Devices	Devices	Devices	Devices	Devices
Applications	Applications	Applications	Applications	Applications
Data	Data	Data	Data	Data
Runtime	Runtime	Runtime	Runtime	Runtime
Middleware	Middleware	Middleware	Middleware	Middleware
O/S	O/S	O/S	O/S	O/S
Virtualization	Virtualization	Virtualization	Virtualization	Virtualization
Servers	Servers	Servers	Servers	Servers
Storage	Storage	Storage	Storage	Storage
Networking	Networking	Networking	Networking	Networking

By Firm	By Vendor

IT as a Service (ITaaS)

IT as a Service completely outsources the entire information technology function to a third party provider. These total service firms handle not only data center operations, but software, local hardware, telephony (usually using voice over IP – VOIP) and can even take care of user devices and printers for a fixed contract price. Each user has a virtual machine (VM) that runs remotely while the local device is simply an input-output mechanism that operates at the lower of the speed of the remote computer or the level of bandwidth. This can be an extremely secure computing architecture for most organizations with the fewest points of vulnerability.

Remote desktop technologies

The current technologies available to businesses today are a far cry from the painful user experiences of the last decades. The most promising for the user experience is the ability to have access to the exact same business applications in exactly the same way on any device without the need for the programming of multiple versions for different operating systems.

Virtual Private Networks (VPNs)

The old way of offering remote workers secure access to company systems was by using a Virtual Private Network (VPN). A VPN established a connection from the users device by creating a virtual point to point connection with tunneling protocols for traffic encryption. This extended the organization's private network onto the internet. This process enabled users to send and receive data across public networks as if their computing devices were directly connected to the private network and each device had all the functionality, security and management policies of the main network. They were secure but unfortunately the method was also painfully slow.

PC-Over-IP (PCOIP) / Virtual Desktop

A remote desktop on either a zero client or any internet capable device is made possible by the PC-Over-IP protocol which transfers an image of software running on a remote server. The PCOIP on the server compresses, encrypts and rapidly transports image pixels to end user devices. The device in turn decrypts, decompress and displays the image on any screen. From the users perspective there is no difference between working with a local computer loaded with software and the zero client (dumb terminal) or handheld device receiving the image of the software running remotely.

Any smart phone, tablet, laptop or desktop machine can become a secure work station as powerful as the main server providing the computing power. In industries in which collaboration is critical but data risk is high, PCOIP offers enhanced protection. Users can collaborate from anywhere knowing that sensitive information never leaves the data center and work can never be physically lost, even if a device is stolen. There are two main types of PC-Over-IP.

Virtual Desktop Infrastructure (VDI)
PCOIP is used to create the virtual desktop that separates the desktop environment and associated application software from the physical device that is used to access it. This approach offers the

most complete disaster recovery strategy because all data is saved in the data center and can be backed up regularly. If the user's device is damaged or lost, recovery is unnecessary because the desktop will be immediately be available from another device with an internet connection. In addition, because nothing is saved directly to the users device, if that device is lost or stolen there is much less chance that any critical data can be retrieved and become compromised.

Remote Desktop Services (RDS)

Remote Desktop Services is a technology from Microsoft Windows Server formally known as Terminal Services. RDS allows the user to take control of the remote computer of a virtual machine over a network connection or the internet. Users view and interact with Remote Desktop Service resources through a proprietary display protocol.

Only the user interface for an application is transferred to the local device. All input from the local device is transmitted to the host server where the actual software execution takes place. This allows the server to host multiple users and desktops at once. The user experience with desktop services may be limited by network bandwidth or remote display protocol capabilities. RDS networks are sometimes less expensive and not as complex as other systems.

VDI versus RDS

Virtual desktop infrastructure is a better choice for small and medium enterprises than remote desktop services for the following eight key reasons.

1. RDS requires an operating system to be running locally. VDI allows for a zero client model which is less expensive and simpler to maintain.

2. RDS requires that all software is the same on all user sessions since the servers are shared by multiple users. For example, if users needed Adobe Acrobat, everyone would need to have the same version and associated licensing. With VDI some users could be licensed for the professional version and the rest for the less expensive or free version.

3. RDS is an older technology where all computing is provided in an environment where every user is sharing resources. The more users that are online the fewer resources each user session has access to. Therefore, if one user is doing heavy processing all other user sessions will suffer reduced performance. With VDI the environment and resources for virtual windows desktop are dedicated to the individual.

4. RDS is run as a server operating system (such as Windows Server 2008 or 2012) and many applications are either not fully compatible or are not built to run efficiently on those systems. VDI, on the other hand, provides a desktop operating system for each user session (such as Windows 10) were all the applications were designed to be run in the first place.

5. Video and sound on RDS systems is often disabled for performance reasons and when available it is usually slow and not optimized for video. VDI allows for superior audio and an improved video experience although multimedia performance is still far inferior when compared to local computing or SaaS products.

6. RDS graphics often seem "choppy." VDI is designed for graphics to be smoother and overcomes common issues with the RDS remote display protocol capabilities previously mentioned. There is still some lag that will occur with VDI but it is not usually significant.

7. VDI offers many more security options. While users in the RDS network connect to the server using a virtual machine (VM) in the same way as with PCOIP the RDS virtual machine is shared with other users and operates on the same server operating system for all users. A breach in one location results in a breach in all of them. VDI is particularly useful when businesses have to deal with critical and confidential data.

8. Printing was designed in VDI to be simpler to manage and more flexible to utilize than in RDS. Both local and network printers are easily accessed with VDI.

In order to determine the strengths and weaknesses of the organization's information technology, management should conduct an analysis of the current infrastructure. There are many ways to accomplish this task. A common tool is a SWOT analysis and the following chapter takes a new look at this traditional method.

A cloud computing SWOT analysis

In a recent meeting in the Chicago loop I was introduced to the TTOWS analysis methodology which is a very clever adaptation of the traditional strengths, weakness, opportunities and threats matrix. It is typical for a disproportionate amount of time to be spent discussing strengths by a group while conducting a traditional SWOT analysis. By the time the organization gets around to the back end of the analysis, which the author considers to be the most important part, the creative and analytical energy of the group is spent.

To concentrate on what is most likely to adversely affect the organization start by reversing the order of analysis and begin not with threats. First look at the overarching trends of the industry as a whole. The descriptions of each of these items may seem to be self-evident and too basic for many readers, but a quick refresher never hurts.

Trends

Examine the trends or external factors that are occurring in society that have the most potential to impact the organization. The best place to start any analysis of an organization's information technology position is with the tech and business world at large in both commercial and business applications. Typical trend questions to focus on include:

- What are we doing now and in what direction is the marketplace moving?

- What is the consensus among the organization's clients, vendors and other stakeholders about the direction that technology is heading?
- How are competitors and clients changing the way they do business?
- What social trends are likely to have an effect on operations?
- What is the legal and legislative environment?

The effect on the information technology structure by social trends such as personal data assistants (PDAs) and subsequently by smartphones and tablets cannot be overstated. Recruiting issues like bring-your-own-device are having a profound effect on the way information technology is going to be handled in the future.

Threats

Threats are external factors that are likely to negatively affect the organization and its key initiatives. Short product cycles in most industries make monitoring trends and tracking the relevant threats from not only market conditions and competitors, but also from the change in mindset of customers and law makers critical.

Opportunities

Opportunities are external factors to the organization that the organization could exploit to its advantage. Realignments that in some circumstances could be threats, such as changing social values or legislation, may also be opportunities. For example, continued media coverage on an issue such as obesity or the fat content of food is an opportunity for the health food industry and a threat to traditional snack food makers.

Weaknesses

These are the internal characteristics that place the organization or project at a disadvantage relative to competitors. Typical weaknesses include information technology infrastructure, data storage and organization and appropriate personnel recruiting, retention management, contracts and other common information technology issues.

Strengths

These are the internal characteristics of the organization or single project that give it an advantage over others in the marketplace. Most organizations can expound on this aspect of the exercise without difficulty so it is best left for last. The examination of the other categories may materially impact the viewpoint of the organization on its strengths.

Sample Cloud Computing TTOWS for and SME

Trends	<ul><li>Installed software replaced by web subscriptions</li><li>Increased customer focus on data security</li><li>Increasing reliance on web based portals to connect with customers vendors and regulators</li><li>Desire for remote work on any device</li></ul>
Threats	<ul><li>Unexpected capital expenditures</li><li>System crashes and data loss</li><li>Unauthorized access to sensitive data</li></ul>

	• Loss of key vendor or employee who understands the current IT system in detail
Opportunities	• Cost savings through better process • Lowered Capex & Opex • Efficient remote access • Improved operational efficiency • Reduced IT manpower cost both internal and vendor
Weaknesses	• Inhouse experience in emerging technologies • Reliance on a key employee/vendor to maintain system • A collection of various hardware devices of varying age and manufacturer utilizing multiple operating systems and software packages of various versions • Aging IT infrastructure, including servers, routers & office devices
Strengths	• Unique value proposition • Core business process and knowledge • Staff expertise • Brand awareness & loyalty • Customer/client service

Now that the varying types of cloud computing options have been examined and a detailed analysis done on the trends, threats, opportunities, weaknesses and strengths of the firm are known the business case for cloud computing can be built.

The business case for the cloud

There is a compelling case for most organizations to move all of their information technology into the cloud by utilizing a holistic approach rather than cobbling together software as a service applications, managed service providers and inhouse resources. Consider that only twenty years ago small and medium size businesses routinely struggled with payroll, sales taxes, court ordered garnishments, distributions, printing checks, preparing and mailing routine payroll and tax forms, managing accounting staff and devising internal controls. This process left business leaders vulnerable to legal risk. Almost all firms now use specialized third party vendors to handle these mundane tasks which lie outside their core competencies. Most organizations trust specialized vendors that are experts in the complex and ever changing laws that cover payroll and taxes.

Information technology is just as complex an issue. Data security, access controls, legal liability, mutating viruses, spam, aging hardware, large upgrade costs, dated software and operating systems, expensive staff and other computer related concerns plague operations of all sizes. Not long ago the only alternative was to have a server in the closet from which mission critical files could be efficiently shared (in theory at least) across the organization. Like payroll, information technology can often be handled more efficiently and at reduced risks and cost by specialized experts.

Strategic considerations

There are a variety of strategic considerations that senior leaders must contend with to determine which cloud computing configuration is the correct one for the organization. The most important of these considerations are discussed in detail.

Lost productivity

The cost of downtime to productivity can be appreciated in the following example. An average fully burdened salary level of $45,000 per employee (assuming that 2080 hours are worked per year) results in an hourly wage of $21.63 per hour.

# Staff	Loss / hour	# Staff	Loss / hour	# Staff	Loss / hour
10	$217	20	$ 533	50	$1081
100	$ 2170	1000	$ 21,770	10000	$ 210,770

The hard cost of lost productivity just in terms of labor cost is easy to calculate but the main concern is that this hard cost is only a small part of the problem.

Revenue and brand damage

Missed business opportunities from both immediate and future sales can have a major impact on not only financial results but also on the opinions of stakeholders. Retailers and sales force personnel trying to close deals before reporting deadlines are hard pressed to succeed if information technology suffers a catastrophic loss that compromises point of sale, quoting tools or the customer management system. A downturn could easily have a domino effect on customers, suppliers and shareholders as was experienced by United.

Lost or damaged data

A crash that results in rework of accomplished jobs has more than just a financial effect on the organization. The damage can easily extend to the firm's reputation and negatively affect employee morale.

Customer dissatisfaction

Even not for profits have customers to serve and the inability to fulfill the organizations' promises can cause serious damage to not only the brand image but also the trust both donors and end users have in the entity.

Delay in returning to normal operation

In the event of a crash how long will it take for the organization to catch up, eliminate backlogs, deal with unsatisfied customers and return to normal operations? The cost of execution can rapidly become significant in terms of opportunity costs and lost revenue in addition to the repairs themselves.

Regulatory & liability risk

Lost data can do far more than cause revenue and brand damage. A crash may have very real regulatory and legal consequences for any size organization. Electronic records stored for compliance purposes such as test requirements or maintained for maintaining not for profit status are particularly problematic. Personnel records and other personally identifiable information that is lost can lead penalties, fees and even lawsuits that result in considerable damage.

In traditional small and medium size business, information technology infrastructure has different platforms running numerous operating systems in various states of repair. Antivirus software, password security, data protection and other mission critical technical issues are often at the mercy of individual users who often work remotely and prefer to use their own equipment. A holistic cloud strategy can help eliminate these concerns by having all the software and data located in one location that users can access regardless of device. Data security is maintained locally because that is stored in only one location which makes its loss or other breaches much less likely.

The simple fact is that the vast majority of security breaches in both the public and private sector have occurred in organizations that have inhouse information technology systems. From the Federal government to top tier public sector organizations and the largest private firms such as Target and Home Depot data breaches are all too common. Even small and medium enterprises are the target of hackers and other malicious threats. If the users of company data in applications can access that information from their desktops laptops tablets and smartphones then the scale of the security issue grows exponentially. By eliminating the vulnerabilities at the device level security is dramatically improved.

A typical small or medium enterprise has various types of computing devices of various ages supplied by multiple manufacturers with multiple operating systems with various configurations. Each of these devices may or may not be running the most up to date version of the operating system or installed software. This fact alone makes it very difficult to maintain a secure environment. Now add the additional complexity of viruses, spam and local passwords and one can get a realistic sense of the vulnerabilities that most firms face.

There is also a very real physical threat. If information is stored locally on the device thieves can easily extract that data from the hard drive as the Veterans Administration learned the hard way when a stolen laptop was compromised. The Social Security Numbers and other personally identifiable information of thousands of veterans, including the authors, was exposed. Even servers are not immune. UC Berkeley lost 8000 student records when a server installed in a closet was stolen from a campus office.

With limited budget and talent to dedicate to security issues and the need to be constantly vigilant and proactive in order to protect valuable data, it is no wonder that data security is such an area of concern for organizations leadership. Limiting the threat to a single point of vulnerability is one of the best ways to secure vital data and prevent embarrassing and potentially devastating losses to the organization.

Information technology as a competitive necessity

The very face of information technology in the workplace has been turned on its head as major obstacles to security, reliability and maintenance that once increased costs and crushed productivity have been eliminated. The cloud offers employees three major advantages over installed software.

1. Work efficiently anywhere

Workers can have the same security, speed, reliability and access to software on any internet device anywhere in the world. Remote workers, outside sales people and traveling executives can have the same user experience and levels of productivity once reserved for their main workspace.

2. Bring your own device

The desire of employees to use a variety of different devices, operating systems and various versions thereof used to be an information technology nightmare. Savvy business leaders now use the freedom to choose any device as a way to recruit both young talent and experienced workers alike. Additionally, the burden of information technology ownership and repair can be passed on to willing employees with no additional security risk to the organization because data and applications are hosted remotely and no data or programs are stored on the personal devices.

3. Mergers & acquisitions

If the organization is considering any kind of Mergers and Acquisition activity, a scalable and fixed-cost technical infrastructure will make both the sale of the business or the absorption of another firm a strength that will add value to the transaction. Once a letter of intent is signed, subpar technology infrastructure is a frequent issue used to justify a negative change in the purchase price. The stability and reliability of information technology will be a major consideration in any due diligence process whether buying or selling.

Procuring IT

Twenty years ago, almost every firm with more than a few employees had someone struggling with the minutia of payroll. Managers would oversee clerks, cut checks, track hours, report to state, local and federal agencies, handle garnishments and court orders and issue W2s and 1099s. Today, almost all businesses with less than 1000 employees outsource payroll according to the Society for Human Resources Management. The main reasons are lower risk and liability, reduced costs and decreased management distraction. Payroll process only matters to most employees when the checks show up late, or worse yet, not at all. Information technology is viewed the same way by the vast majority of users. When payroll is handled by an industry expert that makes the process seamless and performs as needed without effort, business leaders can check one more thing off their task list and focus on mission critical issues.

In the same way that ADP changed payroll, Netflix reinvented movie rentals, Uber transformed livery and airBNB shook up lodging procurement, cloud technology is changing how tech is procured, supplied and managed. The cloud offers a confusing array of pricing and options. The options range from simple tools to complex business information technology. Both extremes are accessed easily by logging into your account from any device anywhere in the world with an internet connection.

Managing growth

Adding a new employee to the organization has always been about as much fun as doing expense reports. The process for information technology onboarding is time consuming and either onerous for inhouse IT personnel or a scheduling issue with vendors. The procedure for everything from installing software, updates and patches to new or reused machines, creating profiles, adding email signatures and other necessary tasks was frequently different for every employee and device.

Even the recruiting and retention process has made the onboarding equation more difficult to solve. Bring your own device used to strike terror into the heart of information technology managers everywhere. Employees in love with their snazzy first addition iPhones were forced to use the company BlackBerry for work in order to ensure the integrity of the network simply because the different operating systems were incompatible.

Rapid growth also brings other information technology issues to light. Storage and speed constraints on servers owned by the organization, whether they are installed locally or remotely, become evident when users are rapidly added to the system. Leaders must guess at capacity needs which may ultimately be much higher or lower than anticipated. If you are like me and also remember the utter nightmare of using an old school VPN in order to access critical business applications or even to look up a prospect in the CRM you may shudder. This made it a challenge to allow employees to work remotely and limited the ability of firms to easily add and then support workers in outside sales and other remote service staff.

Reducing unexpected capital expense

Everything is humming along when the server decides to fry itself into a molten pile of goo. Maybe there was a power surge, maybe there was a manufacturing defect or maybe deferred maintenance led to a catastrophic failure. Regardless of the cause, a crashed server is going to cost a small fortune if information technology is managed inhouse. If the hardware is owned by a third party provider who also manages the equipment, the organization has a resource to rely on in order to fix the problem or according to whatever recovery standards they have negotiated in the contract.

Reducing labor expense

Routine help desk and support are tedious and time consuming. Making sure that printers print and passwords work requires numerous man hours. Onboarding new employees into the information technology infrastructure requires even more. Training users requires yet another set of man hours. These small batches of hours can easily add up.

Let's run a quick calculation. Take a firm that has 50 computer users each potentially with a desktop, laptop, tablet and smart phone. That is more than 200 potential devices. For the sake of argument let's assume the average user has 2.5 devices for a total of 125. Even spending 10 minutes per device, assuming they were all laid out in front of the tech and ready to be worked on, an update or patch would take more than 20 hours. Updates are being pushed for mainstream operating systems and applications with alarming frequency. It is easy to appreciate how managing all of this information technology is ramajor challenge.

Handling internal conflicts with IT staff

Is the information technology staff strategic and critical to the long term success of the business or are they stuck putting out fires, updating software, handling routine complaints or onboarding employees? Question whether they are mired handling these issues themselves or managing staff and coordinating vendors. Using the cloud can eliminate the everyday hassles in routine busywork of information technology and allow staff act strategically and concentrate efforts on growing the business and their careers.

For information technology geeks and the business leaders who need to speak with them, here are a few technical details to consider. First, in order to minimize fear pitch peace of mind. Since system infrastructure is always located in SOC 2 Type II[2] state of the art datacenters, each with redundant power and internet lines, the organization has enterprise level protection against power outages, floods, fire, theft and other catastrophes. The end result for information technology managers is that they will see fewer of,

---

[2] For detailed information on what a typical data center consists of consult https://www.idc-a.org/data-center-standards for detailed information.

if not eliminate completely, those dreaded after hours system alerts. Finally, information technology leaders can leave the office and take weekends and vacations in peace and so can their bosses.

The cost of Information Technology

The typical organization does not have an accurate understanding of the actual cost of their information technology. The following analysis will be conducted with the major elements that a typical enterprise will face and includes both capital and operating expenses. Since the average life span of a server and the associated licenses is approximately three years the analysis is conducted in that time frame. Some organizations will make an information technology investment last far beyond its expected service life with a series of patches and work arounds as detailed previously.

IT capital expenses

The easiest place to start when analyzing true information technology cost is with the capital expenses of a new system with a projected three year life cycle. The analysis will assume that all new installations will occur at a third party server facility for security and reliability reasons as discussed elsewhere. There are three primary areas to consider.

Servers

The purchase of a server to manage the organization's computing power entails significantly more expense and effort than the simple hardware cost of the new server. There are also significant charges for deployment of the system that includes installation, wiring, set up of the various components and software, required security devices, rollover, back up devices and other significant incidentals that can more than exceed hardware cost.

User interfaces

Desktop hardware, dual monitors, large screen smart-televisions for conference rooms, wireless keyboards, mice, laptops, smartphones and desk telephones are staples in every office environment. While the number of remote workers employed by the firm and those team members who prefer to "bring their own device" to use for work may decrease the quantity, the hard cost of hardware is not going to disappear any time soon. Expect the makeup of the hardware to change. The desktop and mobile user interface devices may become inexpensive dumb terminals that communicate with the cloud and be far less expensive than their number crunching predecessors.

Peripherals

The world will never, never, ever be paperless. And I don't mean that in the way Nancy Pelosi predicted the future about candidate Trump. Printers, scanners, chart plotters, projectors and other peripheral devices will remain an integral part of the business landscape until the perfect virtual display device is developed. The fax machine is still alive and well in the guise of the scan to email function on your local office device and that is just another box to connected to the network, maintain and service.

IT operational expenses

Once the capital expense has been determined it is time to consider the ongoing expenses of maintaining the information technology infrastructure. Not all of the expenses that follow are easily identified as technology related on the profit and loss statement.

Some costs are buried in multiple departments or may not be tied directly back to an information technology line item. Nonetheless, it is critical that these expenses are included in analysis in order to make an accurate cost determination of options and keep the information technology guy shouldering his fair share of the expenses.

Internal IT support

Even if the organization does not have a full time position for information technology support, the cost for maintain technology falls somewhere. Managing information technology may fall on a team member as a side project or be the burden of the owner or shifted to an outside vendor. Regardless of how the issues are handled, calculate the man hours spent on these tasks and assign the appropriate dollar value to them.

External IT support

This is one of the easiest line items to calculate, right? Take all of the 1099 vendors and add them up. Not exactly. Many leaders forget to take into account service contracts, purchased tech support hours or priority status and other information technology related expenses. Be sure to check for these expenses in each department to be sure that the various line items are correctly accounted for and applied.

Antivirus & antispam

While the security risks and other implications of virus and spam attacks will be discussed in detail later, there is a hard cost of software and hardware to check for threats and build firewalls.

Training and lost productivity time must also be built in. As fast as new defenses are released a new and craftier virus appears out of the depths of Eurasia from the attic bedroom of a brilliant teenager with a laptop and a pirated Wi-Fi connection. The media abounds with stories of national governments in China, North Korea, Russia Iran and other nations jumping into cyberwarfare and corporate espionage. In the survey of small and medium enterprises leaders that follows, more than one in three respondents reported their organization struggled with spam and viruses on work stations and on other devices in the previous year.

Help desk

There are two ways to deal with the host of small problems that typically arise in any information technology environment. Help desk cost is the time and effort required to handle routine issues like lost passwords, difficulty connecting to the Internet or getting files to print. This expense may come under internal information technology or an external vendor. Beyond a dozen or so employees having access to reliable and timely information technology support is crucial to efficient operations. No organization wants to rely on one staffer to handle these issues and wait for their return from lunch, or worse their return from an overseas vacation, to solve an urgent issue.

Data backup

Business leaders need to be absolutely certain that critical data is being backed up and that is data is readily accessible. According to statistics recently compiled by the Boston Consulting Group, 77%

of businesses discovered significant failures in backup data. The potential for considerable damage to the business is evident.

Recovery & rollover

The main consideration in recovery it the amount of time the leadership team is willing to be without vital business data and applications. Automatic rollover is extremely expensive and requires the maintenance at least one set of duplicate databases, software, licenses and additional switching hardware. The senior leadership team must assess how much downtime the organization can risk.

Depending on the needs of the particular organization down time of any sort maybe be unacceptable. Rollover is very expensive. The amount of bandwidth and systems required to make a seamless transition from the primary to the secondary process can almost double the organization's information technology expenditure. The business must decide how long it organization can afford to be offline. In a high volume retail set up minutes may be catastrophic. Typical business recovery times are typically specified in two hour increments.

Two hour recovery is generally for organizations where is critical to be up as soon as possible without needing the system to automatically roll over. For most groups, a four to six hour window of down time in the event of a catastrophic failure is a reasonable balance between cost and lost productivity. Rollover is an automated process. Other recovery plans rely on labor. In the highly unlikely event that a major disaster occurs at the data center level that affects multiple users simultaneously the difference in recovery time is essentially assignment of the organization in the queue from a labor and available parts standpoint.

Firewall

"Firewall" is a commonly heard and often misunderstood term. A firewall is a security system that monitors and controls incoming and outgoing network traffic based on pre-determined security settings. Network firewalls consist of a software running on the server that filters traffic between two or more networks. Host-based refers to a software firewall residing on a single computer or server. There are also hardware based firewalls that filter traffic between networks.

Routers direct traffic between networks and firewalls are often the point of failure in a network. A router is a networking device that forwards "data packets" between computer networks. Routers essentially direct traffic on the internet. A data packet is typically forwarded from one router to another through the millions of networks that constitute internet until it finally reaches its destination.

The most familiar type of routers are the home and small office varieties that simply pass data such as web pages, email, instant messages and videos between local computers and the internet. The more sophisticated routers connect large businesses and the complex computer systems that run them. Internet service providers forward encrypted data at high speed across the web.

Print and paper

Color printing is expensive no matter which way you cut it. The costs of consumables for these items can easily make output run ten to fifteen cents per page. Those pennies can easily add up to thousands of dollars per year for even very small organizations. This is an expense that frequently gets lost in the P&L as an office supplies expense but should be considered in the creation and tracking of the information technology budget as a way to proactively take control of the budget line and improve the bottom line.

Power consumption

This frequently overlooked aspect of total information technology cost can also easily add up unnoticed in the general overhead or utilities budget line. The power consumption of a typical small office server and the cooling required for it can easily add hundreds of dollars to the utility bill. Standalone computing devices also burn a lot more power than thin clients. My desk contains a laptop with a second monitor, tablet, smartphone and a powered voice over IP phone all running at the same time. This consumes a significant amount of power when multiplied across the entire organization.

Bandwidth

This item was saved for last in the operational cost discussion because it is the one that causes the most confusion and can have the largest direct effect on system performance. Internet access is the backbone of providing the user experience to cloud applications. Software as a Service applications have made a high speed Internet connection as much of a business necessity as the lights. It is a challenge to find any kind of operation that does not already rely on remote computing power in a significant way. Virtually no new or expanding business is installing traditional PBX phone systems. Voice over IP (VOIP) is the new standard. Long distance charges once closely monitored by budget makers is now an inconsequential expense in most organizations and has been replaced by the data pipe.

Rural locations may have only one data choice or no option other than satellite. Urban business are not immune from severe limitations. Choices may be fixed by a landlord who has negotiated binding deals with one provider for a particular property. This is especially common in high rises or in large suburban office complexes.

Regardless of the platform utilized video in all its bandwidth sucking forms must be a serious consideration. Demonstrations, webinars, remote teleconferences and meetings, tech support, interviewing and a host of other common uses are making huge demands on bandwidth. For enterprises that rely heavily on the web and cannot allow any down time it is prudent to consider the installation of two internet providers. One can be the primary high speed line and the second can be a slower connection which act as a failsafe. The organization's firewall can automatically change from the primary to the secondary connection when necessary. If both connections go out, which is very unlikely under most circumstances, or the local power grid has failed completely, staff will be able to access cloud systems from a remote location such as a coffee shop or home office on a different part of the grid.

Mobile device bandwidth

Minutes and gigabytes. Everyone with working senses is bombarded by the messaging of the big cell providers with family and business plans for unlimited talk, text and shared data. Activation fees, early termination fees, two year contracts and a host of other nickel and dime costs may plague these contracts, but the real issue lies in the sheer amount of data that typical user in an organization is going to need. If a user will frequently be accessing a remote desktop from a device via cell networks while traveling or otherwise working remotely, 2 or 3 gigabytes of data will not suffice. A reasonable working number for using a typical remote desktop setup is approximately 1.5 gigabytes per user per eight hour work day. That is a lot of mobile data.

Bandwidth requirement analysis

A typical service organization with twenty normal users in two locations using a common mix of tools can expect to see the following bandwidth usage. Depending on the needs of the organization it is possible that additional bandwidth may be required beyond what is shown here. The use cases in the chart do not take several kinds of heavy remote access data use into account such as that required for high definition graphics, video rendering or other data intensive tasks.

Bandwidth Usage

Usage	Typical	Light	Basic
Web Browsing	√	√	√
Email	√	√	√
Voice	√	√	√
Video Conferencing	√	X	X
Shard Files	√	√	√
Cloud Office Productivity	√	√	√
Cloud Data Backup	√	√	√
Remote Desktop	√	√	X
Upload Speed Required	63.1 Mbps	46.3 Mbps	40.1 Mbps
Download Speed Required	57.4 Mbps	40.6 Mbps	34.3 Mbps

Source: Intergaltelefcom.com bandwidth calculator tool

Finally, the senior leadership team must also consider expenses that are unique to their industry that may include local, state, federal and international regulatory or compliance requirements, insurance for liability and pre-emptive due diligence on systems for mergers and acquisitions.

Total Cost of Ownership (TCO) worksheet

The following worksheet is useful in organizing the various costs associated with the entire information technology infrastructure for most small and medium enterprises.

Using this worksheet

The basis for this worksheet is the total number of seats. Think of a seat as a full time equivalent. Although there may be a one to one correlation between staff and users, in an environment where there are part time workers or shifts access to a seat may be shared.

Capital Expenditures (Capex)	Cost
Server hardware	
Desktop / laptop hardware	
Smartphone hardware	
Peripherals	
Operational Expenses (Opex)	**Cost**
Office bandwidth (internet, phone, video)	
Mobile bandwidth	
IT Support (salary, man hours)	
External IT support	
Antivirus protection	
Anti-spam protection	

Security assessments	
Help desk support	
Data back up	
Recovery	
Recovery testing	
Power consumption	
Print and paper	
Firewall	
Downtime / seat / hour lost	
Server software licensing	
Business software licensing	
Custom software development	
Consulting services	
Software support services	
Other	

The off the cuff estimate

If the worksheet proves to be too onerous to execute or the organizations' leaders require a general idea to calculate the total cost of ownership for comparison purposes, the following per user estimates over the three year life cycle of the typical business server are reasonable estimates. These figures are based on the analysis of hundreds of businesses and the total cost of ownership of information technology systems and staff time allocation per user.

Quick and Dirty Estimator

Item	3 Year	1 Year	Monthly
Server Hardware & Upkeep	$ 945	$ 15	$ 26.25
Desktop Hardware & Upkeep	$ 1350	$ 279	$ 37.50
General Software needs	$ 810	$ 270	$ 22.50
IT Staff / Vendors	$ 2835	$ 945	$ 78.75
Backup / Disaster Recovery	$ 506	$ 169	$ 14
Security (software, consulting)	$ 169	$ 56	$ 4.66
Power	$ 135	$ 45	$ 3.75
Total Cost	*$6750*	*$2250*	*$187.50*

Managed Service Providers

Managed service providers are organizations that are contracted to handle various information technology operations for the business. The managed service provider could offer anything from basic installation and setup of infrastructure either locally or at a data center depending on the needs and the contract. The buyer may still be required to maintain service and support of software, local hardware, mobile devices and even help desk support. Managed Service Providers come in all shapes and sizes and the same due diligence that is used to select a SaaS vendor should be applied here as well.

Cloud Computing Security

The preponderance of literature reviewed identifies critical security issues that stakeholders from the National Command Authority to the average consumer need to consider. These include personal and systemic security measures at every step of cloud computing. There are multiple approaches to securing the cloud and they can be both hardware and software based.

Virtual machines (PCoIP)

PC-Over-IP provides substantial economic and business efficiency benefits but there are a number of significant security concerns that must to be addressed. One example is that there are critical differences between running a virtual machine in an Information Technology as a Service (ITaaS) environment versus running programs and storing data on a local device. The first consideration is that there are the other organizations that are also running virtual machines on the same system. There are major security implications if these instances are not properly isolated. Many systems are susceptible to various vulnerabilities and bugs if not properly configured and maintained. A malicious customer using a co-located virtual machine on the same system may be able to attack these vulnerabilities.

The second consideration is that the software that makes running virtual machines possible has access to all the resources of the system. This access can affect confidentiality, integrity or system availability of the various users. In a cloud computing environment users have no control over this part of the system. This software may also be susceptible to additional bugs and other vulnerabilities.

Consumer cloud security concerns

The general public should be also concerned with cloud computing security issues. Privacy, hacking, theft, cyber-stalking, identity theft, malicious software and child soliciting and abuse are all potential threats to both enterprises and individuals. There are precautions that can be taken to mitigate each of these issues.

Privacy

Public cloud applications allow users to access programs and data on demand at any time, from any location and on any device. In order to allow this kind of uninhibited access users must provide some information. There may be specific requirements of users who may wish to protect their identities. One common example is that using a cloud application to research an illness may reveal the user's identity and provide possible correlations between the illness and that individual or their network. There are techniques that have been developed to keep communication anonymous, but it is incumbent on the user to be familiar with the terms of service and privacy policy of any application they access.

Attribute based access control can be helpful in protecting the privacy of the users. This is a logical access control methodology where authorization to perform a set of operations is determined by evaluating attributes specifically associated with the subject, object and requested operations against stated policies, rules or relationships. In simpler terms, attribute based access control detailed policies and conditions that allow for context sensitive and dynamic security. Variables influencing the process can include time of day, geographic location or attributes of particular users.

Elements of attribute based access control

Policy Store
The policy store is a collection of logical rules and policies that guide access decisions.

Policy Editor
The policy editor is a software tool that allows administrators to create and edit policies that are evaluated and enforced by the decision engine.

Policy Information Point
The policy information point (PIP) encompasses enterprise data stores such as LDAP, MySQL, or Oracle that hold relevant details, or "attributes." Attributes are the data points used to evaluate a user's request against policy.

Policy Decision Service
The policy decision service is an "engine" that evaluates user requests against relevant policies and attributes, renders a decision about access, and triggers appropriate system responses and actions.

Policy Enforcement Point
The policy enforcement point (PEP) intercepts requests for access, and forwards them to the policy decision service for authorization.

(Jericho Systems, 2017)

Hacking

Hacking is the unauthorized access of private or proprietary data. Compromised passwords are the main reason that consumers are the subjects of hacking attacks. Defense against hacking requires more common sense than technology. The same precautions that people have always taken to protect their private information should be applied to the online world. Individuals should not share or write down pins, passwords, social security numbers and other personally identifiable information. Hacking can lead to hijacked accounts, fraudulent bank and credit card transactions and identity theft.

Malicious software

Malicious software, known as malware, is a form of attack where a program is surreptitiously installed on user's system. The most recent version of this attack mode is ransomware by which attackers are able to lock up the infected system and literally hold the content for ransom. The data can only be decrypted after the payoff has been made. There is no guarantee that the hacker will release the data.

A recent global malware cyberattack known as "Wanna Cry" effected 300,000 victims in 150 countries by exploiting a known flaw in Microsoft Windows. Although the flaw had been corrected in a Microsoft update the effected systems had not installed the update and were susceptible to attack. Locally managed systems were hit hard and a ransom paid in untraceable Bitcoin was demanded by the attackers to release the data seized in compromised systems. Fortunately, a kill switch for the malware was found by recent Purdue University graduate and the attack was shutdown.

Most computer users are aware of viruses which can have a variety of effects from criminal intent to simple acts of vandalism. Virus programs can be used to steal usernames and passwords, access data files or simply make the system crash. A common use of infected systems is to stream content or send spam email. There are commercially available security tools that can help scan for these types of attacks and some web browsers and applications attempt to do so or at least identify high risk sites.

Theft

Consumer theft usually involves illegal downloads of movies, games, software, music and other digital files. Services such the defunct Napster and now BitTorrent allow a process called peer-sharing that lets users exchange pirated files that infringe on the copyrights of publishers. The security threat to consumers is that malicious parties can place malware in shared files which can then infect the system the file was downloaded to.

Cyberstalking

Computer users of any age can be stalked online by both the benign and those with wicked intent. Common sense practices will help mitigate most of these concerns. Keeping social media posts private and not posting schedules or similar information that could be used by a stalker will eliminate most of the threat.

Child soliciting and abuse

A major security concern for parents and government officials is the use of the internet and social media cloud applications for facilitating child solicitation and abuse of various kinds. Taking the same precautions as for hacking and stalking and layering adult controls on browsers will limit this risk significantly.

Security threats in the cloud for organizations

There are numerous threats that computing are susceptible to and these vulnerabilities are not necessarily unique to the cloud. Some security threats are magnified by the differences between cloud and local computing while others are mitigated by varying degrees of significance. The main determinant to the severity of that change is how the relative threat is susceptible to remote access.

Data breaches

There have been major data breeches sustained by enterprise level cloud service providers. Vulnerabilities in the vast array of software, hardware and user access points have allowed hackers to gain access to businesses, government agencies and private organizations of every size and type. Although hackers will always be on the prowl for new ways to access secure systems and data, the most common failure point is human error.

Compromised credentials

Compromised credentials are perhaps the most obvious cloud security threat that has increased in importance since the move from local computing. The greatest strength of the cloud, global access, also makes the safety of credentials the most important security consideration. Compromised credentials can allow unauthorized access to systems that may go unnoticed for extended periods of time. No remote system is secure if the attacker has the appropriate passwords.

Phising and other email scams can expose passwords and security questions that can allow hackers access to the assets of an organization. Even a phone call from a blocked number claiming to be customer support can be used to gain access to credentials and compromise systems. There are steps that can be taken to help mitigate this danger. Organizations should implement a robust password policy that mandates frequent password changes. Administrators should verify that all software and hardware default passwords set by the manufacturer have been changed.

Organizations should also mandate two part authentication processes. This is common in banking applications where multiple steps including both username and password combinations combined with a personal identification number or security question are required prior to access. Access to critical information or systems can be limited to particular devices or IP addresses that are pre-approved and authenticated by administrators in advance. All organizations should conduct routine employee training on a recurring basis to ensure that security processes and procedures are familiar and kept at top mind. Finally, frequent scheduled and surprise security audits can be conducted by administrators, managers and contractors.

Hacked interfaces

A hacked interface occurs when unauthorized parties gain access to highly exposed parts of the network that transfer data between systems. This can come through hardware or the application program interfaces (APIs) used to run cloud applications. This is a serious concern. the nature of cloud computing requires that this part of the system be open to constant query from anywhere authorized users wish to have access to the application or data. The security risk increases when third-parties access APIs to build out functionality in their own software as this not only increases the need to expose more services and credentials but also increase the odds that programming errors or other vulnerabilities will occur.

Exploited vulnerabilities

When manufacturer errors or software bugs are not fixed in a timely fashion by the cloud services provider the vulnerability that has not been corrected can be exploited by hackers. The longer the vulnerability remains open the greater the likelihood it will be exploited. Hackers use automated programs call bots to continuously search the web for known vulnerabilities.

Account hijacking

After credentials have been compromised it is possible for a cloud account to be taken over by a hacker. This is also a risk for consumers. The amount of damage that can be caused from a hijacked account is significant. The best defense is maintain strict control over credentials.

Advanced Persistent Threats (APTs)

An advanced persistent data threat is an attack on a computer system that is designed to remain hidden for prolonged periods of time. The hack usually consists of malware that has been installed on a system that infiltrates the architecture by acting like normal system activity. Data can be stolen and manipulated remotely for a variety of criminal reasons.

Nefarious insiders

Any security system is only as good as the people entrusted to operate it. Employees, business partners, contractors and vendors are all potential security threats in any information technology environment, but with cloud computing this risk is especially grave because access can be gained from virtually anywhere. Insiders can easily steal data, install malware or help generate an advance persistent threat. In addition to strong auditing and management practices, providing training to all employees on what to look for will help mitigate the risk.

Permanent data loss

Although unlikely, a potentially catastrophic data security issue with cloud providers is the complete and irrevocable loss of data. Of course, this failure is probably more likely to occur in a self-hosted environment than in a high tech data center, but it is still conceivable.

Poor due diligence

It is incumbent on the leadership team of the contracting organization to thoroughly vet potential vendors. Small firms or those that have had prior security breaches should receive extra attention in the selection process. Organizations that lack the experience internally to evaluate the security risks of providers should consider engaging a consulting firm that can guide them through the process to assure that the acceptable level of risk is contracted for. For internal development, adequate oversight of development and outside contracts must also be closely watched.

Denial of Service attacks (DOS)

Cloud computing is subject to what is known as denial of service attacks. This is a systematic assault on a web server that is designed to make it crash by overloading it with data requests. These requests are often initialed by numerous bots operating simultaneously in a concerted effort by one or more attackers. These attacks are extremely common and can be easily compared to a traffic jam where a lot of cars are all trying to get to one place at one time and movement slows to a crawl or stops completely.

Shared technology

Since the platform of cloud computing service providers is shared among many organizations a compromised vulnerability can affect the entire userbase. The result could be the installation of malware, creation of advance persistent threats, data theft or manipulated transactions. The threat is greatest in cloud applications where there is a shared database.

The threats detailed above are certainly not comprehensive but are representative of those addressed by the major cloud computing security organizations. The World Economic Forum shows concerns of different geographic areas in which the related issues of security compliance, governance and business continuity dramatically outweigh financial considerations. This is a significant finding that clearly demonstrate the value that global businesses place on data security even at the expense of margins and profit.

Ranking risk – industry comparisons

The ten most dangerous cloud computing security risks and their order of precedence depend on the organization compiling the list. The Cloud Security Alliance (CSA), Open Web Application Security Project (OWASP) and the European Union Agency for Network and Information Security (ENISA) have each prepared a ranked list of security threats that they consider the most pressing. It is surprising that all three organizations do not agree on the top threat. Even more surprising, the top ten of each group do not even come close to matching.[3]

For the Cloud Security Alliance the top three issues are the abuse and nefarious use of cloud computing, insecure interfaces and APIs and malicious insiders. The Open Web Application Security Project ranks data ownership, user identity maintenance and regulatory compliance as the three most critical cloud computing security issues. Finally, the European Union Agency for Network and Information Security values data ownership, portability and shared technology risk as the top three issues.

Encryption and access control

Encryption is the process of wrapping a protective layer around data before sending it across the internet or storing the information in a database. Unless compromise the encryption key is only known to authorized users and this technique is usually adequate to protect the data against unauthorized access. Concerns on the security

---

[3] A comparative chart of the risk factors and their relative ranking can be found at https://www.isaca.org/Journal/archives/2012/Volume-5/Pages/Cloud-Risk-10-Principles-and-a-Framework-for-Assessment.aspx

and confidentiality of outsourced data storage has been one of the main issues studied in cloud computing and was the principle deterrent to cloud computing adoption. Data protection can be successfully accomplished using encryption and fragmentation either singularly or in combination. It is important to consider that when data is encrypted it becomes very difficult to execute queries of databases.

Selective Encryption: Various users may require different privileges on information stored in the cloud. Because of the nature of the cloud, efficiency precludes the data owner from maintaining access controls while privacy prevents the server storing the data to enforce them. One solution is to utilize selective encryption where different keys are used for encrypting different data for authorized groups of users.

Cryptographic key management

Cryptographic key management is a critical part of cloud security. Key management should use protocols that are widely accepted and have been extensively vetted through a rigorous review process. Some of these protocols include the National Institutes of Standards and Technology's FIPS (Federal Information Processing Standards) and the Internet Engineering Task Force (IETF) Secure Shell (SSH) and Transport Layer Security (TLS).

Security Process Recommendations

In order for firms to mitigate risks there are processes that can be performed using industry guidance to minimize them.

Cloud Security Assessment

The Cloud Security Alliance (CSA) provides a free STAR Self-Assessment that can be used to document compliance with the organization's best practices. The process commenced in 2011 and cloud computing organizations including Amazon Web Services, Hewlett-Packard, Microsoft and many others have participated. The Cloud Security Alliance has two types of reports that can be submitted.

"Cloud providers can submit two different types of reports to indicate their compliance with CSA best practices:

1. The Consensus Assessments Initiative Questionnaire (CAIQ), which provides industry-accepted ways to document what security controls exist in IaaS, PaaS and SaaS offerings. The questionnaire (CAIQ) provides a set of over 140 questions a cloud consumer and cloud auditor may wish to ask of a cloud provider. Providers may opt to submit a completed Consensus Assessments Initiative Questionnaire.

2. The Cloud Controls Matrix (CCM), which provides a controls framework that gives detailed understanding of security concepts and principles that are aligned to the Cloud Security Alliance guidance in 13 domains. As a framework, the CSA CCM provides organizations with the needed structure, detail and clarity relating

to information security tailored to the cloud industry. Providers may choose to submit a report documenting compliance with Cloud Controls Matrix."

Organizations can ask potential vendors if they have completed one of these two assessments as part of the due diligence process or use the questions as the basis for their own evaluation of potential cloud service providers. Although we have identified that the CSA's most critical aspects and ranking of cloud computing security may differ from that of other organizations, the overall content is relevant regardless of priority assigned. Rankings will vary on an organization by organization basis based on risk tolerance, budget and mission requirements.

Cloud Standards Customer Council

The Cloud Standards Customer Council (CSCC) has published Security for Cloud Computing Ten Steps to Ensure Success Version 2.0 "to provide a practical reference to help enterprise information technology (IT) and business decision makers analyze the security implications of cloud computing on their business." The document provides relevant guidance on the cloud security landscape and includes security guidance and a security assessment section.

Controls for Securing Data

The Cloud Standards Customer Council suggests five major steps customers should take to help mitigate risk to data in a cloud computing environment by assuring data is secure. These tasks can be accomplished using either in house personnel or outside vendors.

- Create a data asset log
- Consider all forms of data
- Consider privacy requirements
- Apply confidentiality, integrity and availability procedures: this includes encryption keys, algorithms, backups and other processes.
- Apply identity and access management

The CSCC's Cloud Security Assessment contains eight sections of questions that organizations need to consider in their selection and utilization of cloud computing services. The eight sections covered in the assessment are:

1. Effective governance, risk and compliance
2. Proper reporting of operations and business process
3. Managing roles and identities
4. Data protection
5. Privacy
6. Security provisions
7. Network and connection security
8. Cloud service agreements

There are numerous specific questions to be asked in each category that are beyond the scope of this discussion. The concerns expressed by the Cloud Standards Customer Council may not rank in the same order as the match those of the Open Web Application Security Project, Cloud Security Alliance or the European Union Agency for Network and Information Security but the same content is covered in each. Ultimately, it will be up to the senior leadership team as to what issues will be most important based on the mission and priorities of the stakeholders.

Legislative concerns on security

Depending on the nature of the cloud computing applications being utilized there may be additional security requirements mandated by the jurisdictions in which the firm operates. The regulatory requirements regarding privacy and data collection of personally identifiable information vary widely between the United States and The European Union, the latter being much more stringent in its restrictions of what organizations may and may not collect.

It is important for organizations to consider that regulations of a particular industry may apply to them even if they do not operate in that market. A stark example of this is the Health Insurance Portability and Accountability Act (HIPAA) that applies to companies that store health and insurance related information about employees and their families. Firms that fail to comply with data protection requirements face a number of consequences including the potential for fines by one or more government agencies or industry regulators. Organizations that use cloud services providers must ensure all legal or regulatory requirements that are applicable to the firm are being executed by the vendor. It is the organization's responsibility, and not that of the provider, for compliance irregularities.

In addition to exposing the firm up to a public relations nightmare, data security issues can spur costly lawsuits that may lead to civil damages and punitive fines. Legal issues will also distract management and information technology personnel, potentially for years. Businesses that provide cloud computing services of any type (hybrid, private, public) and those that consume those services must consider what the potential consequences will be in the event of a breach, loss of data or violation of applicable laws in the various jurisdictions. With the global nature of the web and e-commerce borders have significantly less relevance and firms may potentially be under the requirements of hundreds if not thousands of jurisdictions of local, state, provincial and national bureaucracies. Laws will likely vary on how determinations are made on basic issues such as where the personal data is legally located and which party is responsible for processing.

The Cloud in 2017

What do the leaders of small and medium enterprises really understand about the way that their organizations use IT? The answer is an interesting mix of contradictory opinions. Business leaders struggle with many technology related issues and cloud computing is no exception. In proprietary research conducted by the author in December of 2016 and January of 2017, 576 senior level executives in a variety of enterprises in both public and private sector were survey via phone and asked a series of yes / no / I don't know questions.

The results were fairly predictable but there were also some questions that yielded some very unexpected responses. The levels of satisfaction among business leaders on the overall state of their information technology infrastructures was surprisingly high even as the same executives reported significant pain points. Highlights from the 2017 survey results that are most illuminating follow.

Despite self-reported high levels of satisfaction, it is very unlikely that these levels reflect the actual safety, efficiency and cost effectiveness of the respondents information technology infrastructure. As long as things are working well enough there is very little incentive for senior business leaders to look under the hood for the possibility of discovering incremental gain or a possible unexpected expense. Unfortunately, what is being ignored may have profound consequences.

2017 Cloud Computing Survey

597	Targeted respondents answered a series of yes / no questions
89 %	Had titles of President, CFO, VP, CMO, CTO or Director
203	The average number of FTE computer users in the organization
81 %	Reported keeping business data in the cloud
96 %	Experienced "significant" downtime or other IT issue
1 in 10	9% reported having experienced some kind of data breach
1 in 4	Reported not using a SaaS, but 92% responded yes to a product mentioned by name
1 in 2	Complained that working remotely was difficult
90 %	Satisfied with current IT and 8 in 10 feel comfortable with security and business continuity

There is still a large amount of confusion about how business leaders understand the cloud. To be very clear any software where the computing power resides off site is considered to be in the cloud. Does the organization use LinkedIn to stay in touch with clients and prospects? Google Docs, Adwords or Gmail? If so, the business has data that is stored in the cloud.

It has been the author's experience that what executives are told about the state of their technology may or may not be completely accurate. The frequency, efficacy and reliability of backup and recovery plans are often overstated. Three in four of the respondents reported that backups were being made, backups were current and data restoration plans had been tested. Even if the survey results are materially true, which is statistically very unlikely, the question was created to measure perception of non-technical leaders not looking for the reality of the situation. Even if accurate, one out of every four business leaders thinks that their crucial business data is at risk. In practice, the actual risk is likely gravely understated recalling the Boston Reporting Group finding that 77% of backups have serious issues.

Getting Started

In order to start the organization's journey into the cloud the first step is to assess the current state of the existing infrastructure. This process is not as daunting as it may first appear. A sample discovery process follows that reviews fundamentals, objectives, areas to be assessed and finally a network and process overview.

Fundamentals

In order to minimize risk and expense it is critical to gain a clear understanding of the organization's information technology issues that affect performance, security and remote accessibility. At the conclusion of a network assessment and discovery process the organization will be able to identify that the correct core issues which fundamentally effective the organization's information technology are being appropriately addressed. The management team needs to have complete transparency to any changes or issues which could potentially result in a cascading system failure. These casualties are difficult to troubleshoot and resolve after the fact.

Objectives

The objectives of the network assessment and discovery process are straight forward and necessary. To be certain that the correct solutions are being considered the process must include the following at a minimum. First, an objective review of the organization's infrastructure environment in order to gauge current functionality performance and risk. Second, an analysis is conducted to determine the system's ability to meet the business requirements both at present and in the foreseeable future. Third, it is necessary to document the current information technology state to act as a baseline for creation of a plan for the implementation to a new information technology structure.

Areas to be assessed

A successful network assessment discovery process has two main components. Whether the review is conducted with internal staff or external resources, leverage multiple viewpoints to provide the most objective result. The first step is stakeholder engagement. This process includes a detailed survey analysis of the organizations expectation management physical site and cabling infrastructure second technical analysis of network devices and applications.

Network assessment and discovery

A useful network assessment and discovery process will include the following steps. First, in depth interviews of all stakeholders will be used to define the business goals that must be addressed by the project. Second, extensive testing and analysis of the current information technology infrastructure should cover the following points: physical hardware health, network capacity, network throughput, network latency and cost analysis.

Third, the organization needs To collect detailed information on device performance. The assessment should cover the following areas and occur for all office location including server and workstation computers, network infrastructure, availability needs, business continuity requirements, internet services and connectivity, remote access and thin client computing needs. Additional areas for review include the messaging environment, backup and disaster recovery requirements, security (both internal and external), spyware, virus and Trojan horse protection and finally software license compliance.

Fourth, the assessment should create measurement reports that clearly explain the issues discovered and the order in which they need to be addressed. Fifth, a final assessment must be created and that document should be used to make recommendations to guide decisions on priorities for both implementation and improvement of the current information technology infrastructure.

Finally, a clear and detailed presentation of findings to all stakeholders must be made which details the results of the network assessment in detail. This provides a clear overview of the discovery process so the organization's strategic leaders receive accurate information that provides clear guidance and avoids technical jargon about the findings and what those findings indicate are best for the business. This document should provide at least the following five data points.

1. A review of the existing infrastructure and known issues
2. A review and analysis based on the results of the testing process
3. Network diagrams that correctly specify the issues to be resolved
4. Results of performance measurements
5. Recommendations for remediation and implementation

The resulting recommendations derived from the network assessment in the discovery process will enable the customer to create clear and accurate understanding of the current network. The information is used as a basis for planning and troubleshooting existing systems.

Cloud Migration Considerations

Service Level Agreement	What amount of downtime can be risked?
Upfront cost	What are the relative startup costs by vendor?
Backup level	How much data loss can be risked?
Recovery level	How much down time can be risked?
Security	<ul><li>Mobile device security</li><li>Encryption</li><li>Security management</li><li>Identity & access management</li><li>Access monitoring</li><li>Breach detection & reporting</li><li>Attribute based access controls</li></ul>

Confidentiality	What standards the does the vendor's datacenter and internal compliance meet?
Bandwidth requirements	What will local and mobile bandwidths requirements be and what options are locally or contractually available? Is telephony included in this figure?
Bring your own device	Can users provide they own hardware and securely access the system?
Exit strategy & cost	What are the hard costs and downtime to encountered with a change in vendor?
Support	Who will manage support? What response time is guaranteed? What is the escalation policy? Where does the firm fall in terms of client priority?
Help desk	Who provides basic help desk functions? (passwords, printer issues, etc.)
Updates	What level of maintenance is provided by the vendor?

Compliance	What standards the does the vendor's datacenter and internal compliance meet?
Scalability	How rapidly and reliably can users and data capacity be added or removed from the system?
Software	Is the firm familiar with the support requirements of your applications? Who will act as the liaison?
Miscellaneous	Will onsite support be required? Will telephony be required as part of the contract?

Although the outline above is by no means extensive, it does give the non-technical side of the leadership team a basic list of issues to review.

Conclusion

Although there are significant documented risks involved with cloud computing the advantages to the marketplace far outweigh any security concerns. Most of the security issues that are raised in the cloud have a matching concern in local computer processing. The major differences between the two are global accessibility and the expanding use of third parties accessing application program interfaces and other network connections that expand the opportunities for systemic failure. The ability of hackers to penetrate multiple users at one time by exploiting vulnerabilities in the cloud computing environment is significant but can be effectively managed by both providers and end users.

One final consideration for managers and administrators in the development of cloud computing security plans is that security controls, additional process management, incident response drills and plans and staff training are not free. There are hard and opportunity costs involved with implementation. Not only do increased security requirements require additional bandwidth, there is a demonstrated difference in cost between different levels of encryption. As the level of security increases the level of usability decreases in turn. Organizations must find a balance. For government agencies and organizations dealing with national security or health issues the tolerance for risk may be much lower than a photo sharing application. Even then, the public fallout of hacks can be significant so all cloud applications must make security a principle concern in every aspect of their operations.

As part of the risk calculation cloud service providers can consider the opportunity cost of clients to switch providers. If an organization has built its business model on the vendor's service offering it may be almost impossible for the client to make any sort of architectural change without suffering catastrophic financial loss. This reality may prove a disincentive to certain businesses in low growth areas to invest as heavily as they may otherwise be required to provide the best available security.

Risk tolerance in the marketplace is fluid and will determine which of the security concerns addressed by the Cloud Standards Customer Council, Open Web Application Security Project, Cloud Security Alliance or the European Union Agency for Network and Information Security will be prioritized. Alternatively, it is very possible that whatever the most recent sensational attack that gathers significant press and social media attention will be given priority until the next big issues emerges. The best course of action for cloud computing security practitioners and stakeholders will be to address the needs of their constituents and assess the organization's level of risk tolerance and required operational efficiency to develop a security plan that compromises between those needs.

There is of course still the traditional option which entails the most risk and expense. There are still some firms that have decided to maintain most aspects of their information technology function inhouse with the obvious exceptions of large scale shared public items like the internet connection and power generation. A quick web search will reveal that the highest number of data breaches in every sector (including all levels of government, banks, retail, education, not for profits, legal practices and others who would likely be the most secure) have occurred at organizations that maintain proprietary information technology systems. There is only so much capital for upgrades and limited world-class technology talent to go around. Those firms that have made do with less than state of the art equipment and tolerated deferred maintenance have routinely paid a heavy price in both financial and intangible costs.

Information technology outstanding and even desktop virtualization has become a viable option for organizations which are required to optimize the limited resources provided, ensure a quality remote user experience and deliver ever higher levels of performance in order to stay competitive. Organizational leaders are fortunate in today's information technology environment compared to their predecessors. While the last generation of managers struggled with a rapidly changing hardware and software environment that made technology decisions obsolete before they were implemented, today's leaders can take comfort in the fact that the preponderance of the information technology burden and corresponding risk is once again being shifted outside of the enterprise.

Software as a Service and other technology providers are responsible for the myriad of complex and contradictory changes that come rolling daily out of Redmond, Silicon Valley, Rochester, and other tech centers. As processing power, security, virus and spam concerns continue to shift outward, enterprises of all sizes can reallocate critical management effort to strategic concerns.

The end result of the importance of information technology and security to the overall health of the company has made for a dramatic change for the role of information technology leaders in the senior leadership team and the boardroom. Twenty or thirty years ago, for those of us old enough to remember, payroll outsourcing firms came to organizations and offered to absorb all the fulfillment requirements of the payroll process. These services handle tax payments, reporting to federal, state and local authorities, W2 and 1099 preparation and distribution, garnishments, benefits another operational details. That allowed finance leaders to become less technical and more strategic in their roles.

Today, outsourcing this function is the norm, and information technology is rapidly headed in the same direction. While an organization's information technology management may initially resist adopting a cloud model (which at first glance may seem like a diminishing of their role) in the end it will make these staffers more valuable as they become less tactical participants in the enterprise. The ability for a finance guy to become chief executive officer was almost unheard of when I started in business but this is a common occurrence today. The reason is simple.

Finance staff time was shifted from the management of routine tasks and their skillset was applied to focus on developing strategic analysis and implementation. Additionally, the front line tech jobs are never going to go away, they are just going to exist in a different location.

As small and medium enterprises examine the evolving landscape from the security and audit requirements of their clients to multi-jurisdictional regulation and compliance they must determine what level of managerial effort they wish to dedicate to information technology, how much capital they wish to invest in technology and how much risk the organization is willing to take on. Information technology was often seen through the lens of being a competitive advantage for firms that took were able to invest heavily and apply best practices. Today, when expense risk and effort around technology are examined holistically, the right strategy based on the organization's needs is more likely to be a prerequisite for survival.

Select Bibliography

Cloud Computing Security. TechTarget.
http://searchcompliance.techtarget.com /definition/cloud-computing-security

Cloud Security Alliance. About CSA STAR Self-Assessment.
https://cloudsecurityalliance.org/star/self-assessment/#_overview

Jajodia, Sushil (2014). Secure Cloud Computing. New York:
Springer.

Lovejoy, Ben. (24 February 2017). Cloudflare security breach
exposes data from Uber, Fitbit, OKCupid among 3,400 websites;
password changes recommended.
https://9to5mac.com/2017/02/24/cloudflare-server-breach-cloudbleed-uber-fitbit-okcupid/.

Michelson, James. (2017) Cross Media Marketing 101.
Indianapolis: Schooner Press.

Rashid, Fahmida. 11 March 2016. The dirty dozen: 12 cloud
security threats.
InfoWorld.http://www.infoworld.com/article/3041078/security/the-dirty-dozen-12-cloud-security-threats.html

Security for Cloud Computing Ten Steps to Ensure Success
Version 2.0. (March 2015). Cloud Standards Consumer Council.
http://www.cloud-council.org/deliverables   /CSCC-Security-for-Cloud-Computing-10-Steps-to-Ensure-Success.pdf

Thee, Harrison. (2016) Little Book of Cloud Computing.
Indianapolis: Schooner Press.

Vohradsky, David. (n.d.). Cloud Risk—10 Principles and a
Framework for Assessment.
https://www.isaca.org/Journal/archives/2012/Volume-5/Pages/Cloud-Risk-10-Principles-and-a-Framework-for-Assessment.aspx

About the Author

James Michelson is a former Naval Officer and Professor and has experience in recruiting, hiring, training and leading sales and marketing teams with the Fortune 15, small corporations, and entrepreneurial start-ups in both technology and agency worlds. His specialty lies in creating marketing and sales programs that support the successful prosecution of long cycle and complex consultative business to business sales processes for technology, engineering, plans and assessments and a variety of luxury and consumer products.

Strategic Planning & Marketing Implementation

Revenue cures all ills, and great content & delivery drives revenue before the sales process starts

Planning, project management, support and execution of the following critical processes is available:

Content Strategy	Marketing Automation	Lead Generation
Vision	Strategy & Planning	List development
Copywriting	Systems Selection	Re-engagement
Editing	Funnel Development	Affiliate, Dealer & VAR Networks
Execution	Content & Delivery	Compliance

Web & Social Media	Retention & Conversion	Planning & Strategy
Strategy & Focus	Membership	Product Development
Functional Specifications	Engagement	Market Research
Platform Selection	Referral Engines	Competitve Analysis
PPC / PPM / SEO	Lifetime Value	Budget and P&L

Visit www.jmichelsomn.com for more information, articles and videos and a complete portfolio of completed projects.